JERUSALEM BREEZES

JERUSALEM BREEZES

A Human Panorama of Jerusalem
and a Hope for Peace

by Michel M. J. Shore

SHENGOLD PUBLISHERS, INC.
New York

ISBN 0-88400-079-6

Library of Congress Catalog Card Number: 81-84026

Published by Shengold Publishers, Inc.

23 W. 45th St., New York, N.Y. 10036

Printed in the United States of America

Dedicated to the memory of my father
Sigmond Shore
A Noble and Fine
Man of Word

This book evolved from the ten months (April 13–February 13, 1977–1978) which I spent in Israel with my wife Barbara and my daughter Betty (my son was born in November, 1978). Some dreams and certain experiences of actual previous visits or daily mental walks taken in Jerusalem wherever I am in the world, encounters, longings, thoughts, prayers, hymns of praise to God, are always centered geographically, historically within the all encompassing spirituality of Jerusalem.

Jerusalem is a place, a time (for all time), an atmosphere, an event that . . .

INTRODUCTION

Just as Jerusalem, set within a geographic panorama of hills, mountains, valleys, filled with sunshine or clouds, suggests at different moments ruggedness and gentleness, lushness and barrenness; so too the human panorama of that city seems ever-changing. Gentle breezes or harsh, gusting winds, benevolent sunlight or flooding rain sweep the gallery of portraits etched within the soul. Wild flowers and newly planted gardens complement the landscape of the character of its inhabitants. The contrasting settings, smells, sounds, decor and music are and always will be Jerusalem. The city is itself a part of every Jerusalemite. And who is a Jerusalemite? Anyone who has ever been touched by the city, whether he lives in it or it lives in him.

TABLE OF CONTENTS

THE DANCING EYES, THE WHITE STARCHED TABLECLOTH AND THE BLAZING AFTERNOON

THE DANCING EYES, THE WHITE STARCHED TABLECLOTH AND THE BLAZING AFTERNOON

The white starched tablecloth was set on a surface that be-
ʟayed it. Neither was it a dining room table nor a kitchen table;
for it was too large for a kitchen and yet too small for a dining
room, which was in any case nonexistent there. It simply was
what it was, a table, like many in Jerusalem, waiting for guests,
for a celebration, for a holiday—an excuse to be covered with
napkins, silver cutlery from an era and a country far away. The
three crystal glasses added to the light in the room. Although the
venetian blinds were drawn, the clear, starry globlets, seemed to
have found their own source of light. A few wild flowers adorned
a Yar-zeit glass with shades of yellow, red and bright orange.
Some bottles of liquor and a flask of wine, neatly lined in a row,
bespoke hospitality. The white stone floor was spotless, glimmer-
ing with a sheen, as if each slab had been polished with a velvet
cloth.

An inviting smell of chicken soup intermingled with the fragrance of a freshly-baked cake wafted through the opening of the
kitchen door. Sounds of children playing a few storeys below, in
a nearby playground, entered the small apartment, even though
every window was closed in order to shut out the blazing midday
heat.

It was a small apartment, as could be seen at a glance: the hall
with the ready-in-waiting, set table; a bedroom to the left in
which a small bed adorned with a silken red cover gave it the ap-

pearance of yet another room, which it was and which it wasn't and to the right a small den with a sofa for three which could seat two comfortably, and two light-weight armchairs of a kibbutz-fabrication surrounded a coffee table made at the same collective settlement. In the far left of this room, an efficient looking table held a moderately large wine-red lamp from a by-gone era which might have had a Limoges stamp under its base. Wine red was definitely the theme color, carefully chosen to hold the lamp, as well as for the coffee table. A rather large serviette of that color, rectangular in shape, gave the room warmth. What it lacked in massive comfort, it made up in a small and yet carefully thought out coziness. A music box made of olive wood, a typical work-shop product of one of the northern kibbutzim, waited to be wound.

She stood determined, yet looking so fine and delicate, a small woman, eyeing me from the door as I ran up the stairs, chocolate in hand, perspiration dripping down my face. A pleasant French perfume scent touched my nostrils—it was an introduction to a homecoming. Her eyes were dancing with life, her mouth wrapped a smile as if it were a gift decorated with a pretty ribbon, the theme color of the apartment. As the eyes were her dominant feature, it took a long while to focus on the high expressive forehead, which was lined, eyebrows, chin, lined neck. And, yet such smooth cheeks, of such a soft complexion. The arms were of the same texture. Only in the hand and fingers, did I see more lines. It might have been there that her story began many years ago. If the hands could speak, I thought, each line would relate a different chapter of her incredible life.

I entered, closed the door, was kissed and kissed the beautiful cheeks, was captured by the brillant eyes which seemed to say, "The ankles, which you noticed—the varicose veins are only an illusion."

I was embarrassed. I felt that I should stay the afternoon, knowing full well I had intended to visit for only an hour. I had eaten a sandwich a short while ago, an ersatz lunch, a notion of saving time transported with me from a western hurried society, which, more often than not, ran into conflict with the wishes of my inner being. I immediately began by saying how sorry I was that she had gone to so much trouble, as I was staying for a short while but would be back soon, soon and often.

The eyes did not stop sparkling, nor was there a trace of visible displeasure in them. Rather, I sensed a certain resignation, as if this was not the first time she had waited fruitlessly to spend a few hours of reminiscence, so that someone would have, if not a detailed chronological account, at least a taste of what life had been like, so that the story, hers, his, theirs, ours, would be kept somehow, somewhere.

She lived alone. She would never hear of living anywhere else. Her husband had died many years ago, in a different land and era. She had raised a son, now a scientist, married with two boys, whose family pictures held places of prominence in both the makeshift dining room and the den. Her contact with her son was via his infrequent aerogrammes and her frequent letters. His was a busy life of research, seminars, publications, family; hers a life which never appeared occupied to anyone who entered it and yet, upon reflection, never fell into repose.

The starched cloth napkins which had been so neatly folded like small Napoleon hats were now reclining witnesses to a sumptuous meal, simple in substance and yet elegantly prepared, with chicken dressed in parsley, a salad decorated with prettily cut radishes, a lemon sponge cake dripping with strawberries, and the inevitable *Lehaim* glass of wine. There was an extra glass and place setting for anyone else who might enter.

I had said nothing new—I spoke of everything and nothing, of everyone and no one. She always gave me something to take with me: a memory of something she had done or witnessed, or was about to do, not to mention the present she always had tucked away. I could never leave empty-handed. She would look around her abode, furtively, for something that might be of use, give me pleasure, or that someone I knew might fancy. I never declined her gifts—for they were an extension of her. As she went out to find this day's trophy, my eyes roamed over the spines of her books: a Bible, English grammars, Hebrew novels, Hebrew Ulpan Teaching Manuals which showed signs of much use by new immigrants she had volunteered to teach, a few ledger notebooks and a tattered volume, on which one could still discern the title *Accounting Methods.* The latter somehow looked out of place; they belonged more on her government desk, cleared at mandatory retirement age. There were volumes of English literature, yet so little in her own maternal Polish. Her ancestral Hebrew won out, as did Shakespeare's plays. As always, I thought of how her son's medical scientific university texts bespoke a time which had come and gone, of coffee which she had brewed while he was studying for exams, with results which bore prizes, honors, travel abroad, a career and . . .

Ah, she had found it. This time I would walk out with the music box, in its original plastic container, which had been appropriately put aside with strings and cards. A wish accompanied the gift. "May you hear music wherever you go."

Before letting me leave, she announced that she would be able to be in my company just a little longer, as she was immediately going out after putting away the perishables. Although she was not in the habit of leaving her dishes, she wanted to visit the mother-in-law of her brother at the old age home. The woman had been depressed the night before, and if she could have a piece of cake while afternoon tea was being served, it might make a difference. The strawberries! She would bring the rest of the basket and perhaps prepare a quick jam in the home's kitchen.

Out we went, I with my small present in my hand, she with cake and strawberries in a large plastic bag which I was not to carry. It was she, as she stated, who would have to carry it further in any case, and she was used to carrying things; she did not want to become spoiled. As you can well imagine by now, insist as I might have, I could not spoil her.

The heat of the day had not dissipated during my short visit.

The sunshine set ablaze every corner of the street. A sought-for breeze was nowhere in the vicinity. Her elegant straw hat shaded her kindly radiant face. My remark about the heat and her walking in it with package in hands, brought only the following retort: "Remember that the city is Jerusalem, and that it is summer, and if you want to be well, walking in its streets, you will need a hat."

Rehov Haporzim is a small street near Palmah, a few streets away from Jabotinsky. Each piece of land, or I should say each plot of sand, is watered with what little water has been alloted to it, so that in spring, flowers carpet the parched ground that rarely shows a blade of grass in summer. The air was still, the tranquility lulled us to walk and talk most softly in order not to disturb the silence which covered the street. It was the hour for children to nap, while their parents performed small chores. Only a distant Chopin sonata accompanied us on our walk, an occasional car passing by. Once a baby who had inappropriately awakened cried out. The dusty road, strewn with rocks and chalk-white pebbles, scuffed my shoes. By contrast, her white Oxfords seemed to blend into the surroundings, her feet moving surely, with a determination which had long since substituted itself for youth and a vigour which was of the spirit.

She loved and knew every stone, she said. Indeed, neither the discomfort of the afternoon, nor the intention which had brought her into it could stop her from explaining the significance of the name of the district, Katamon, where David had fought the Philistines. Having studied Greek in high school she was happy she could put it to use. "The name, Katamon, is a shortened Greek term for 'next to the monastery,' and indeed next to the St. Simeon monastery is a pine grove."

Walking further, we came to the Valley of Rephaim, where one of David's greatest victories took place. "The story," she told me, "as you know, is in the book of Samuel (II Sam. 17-25). It was there that David, newly appointed King, won a major battle and saved the Israelites. This battle was recalled by the people hundreds of years afterwards when Isaiah evoked it: 'For the

Lord shall rise up as in Mount Perazim...' (Isaiah 28:21). The valley is named after the Raphaim, a tribe of giants who roamed the country in very ancient times. The stone tools of prehistoric man have been found there.''

To be assured that I would not lose my way, she pointed out to me the direction of the western slope of the Katamon, to where Kefar Goldstein, the youth village was situated, my residence with my students. And then we parted. I kissed her pleasant face and right lined hand, promising that I would buy a hat that very day when the stores reopened at the end of the siesta, which in Israel is called *hafsaka*.

DAWN IN EIN KEREM

DAWN IN EIN KEREM

We stood at the door. She was a beautiful woman, delicately featured, with perfectly formed lips, high, intriguing cheek bones, inquiring, playful yet somehow also serious eyes; they were as blue as the Mediterranean on a sunny day. Small, finely featured ears, behind which her very long, soft sandy-blond hair had been placed in a simultaneous reflex movement of both hands, so as to brush back not only her hair but to push aside sleep at dawn. The baby had cried out several times at night, and not wanting to awaken her husband, she had not allowed herself to fall into a deep slumber. He needed his rest; he would have a long day, just like all the others that did not fall on Shabbat or the awaited holiday. His demanding crisis management job (it seemed that the Party was always in crisis), his full time university program which he had entered after years of financial deprivation, and the technical school classes he taught in the evenings required a complete restoration of energy. It was good to have him at home, in any case. The ever-looming *Miluim,* reserve duty, was either just finished or about to begin, requiring a rescheduling of all his activities. She was used to it, of course. Having been in the country for a number of years, it was like her breathing in and breathing out, simply there, and as a result not there.

One would have never known that she was shortly expecting a baby. Her robe was voluminous. In saying goodbye, I could not help but notice her lovely sculptured forehead, that of a thinking being. I wanted to leave hastily as her feet were bare and the cold stone floor made her shiver once or twice. I had declined breakfast, stating that I wanted to go to my apartment to pick up a briefcase before going to an early morning meeting. Taking her shapely hands, chapped by too many dishes washed and too few gloves worn—a typical carelessness about her own well-being—I thanked her for the sumptuous meal the previous night, for having been allowed to play with the baby past its usual bed-time, so that she could prepare the supper which she thought befitted a good friend who had to stay in town to work, while his wife and child were on a short, *tiyul* excursion. In short, I thanked her for having treated me royally. I asked that she thank her husband once more for having stayed up much later than usual so that we could talk, listen to old and new songs on the phonograph, and dream our dreams of Jerusalem, for the realization of which we both hoped and worked.

I walked out, kissing the mezzuzah, waving goodbye, and caught a warm parting smile. I felt the December chill. The sun had not yet had time to do its work. I buttoned my coat and wrapped my scarf closer to my neck and throat.

I was greeted by the morning and the quietude of a city that in its eternity was awakening again. I could now see clearly that which the shadows of sunset and the curtains of the night had concealed as a surprise. For all I could see the previous evening, when uttering the Minha and Mariv (afternoon and evening) prayers from the balcony of the house I had just left, was the backdrop of the mountains, which included Mount Herzl and the Memorial Mount, and the menorahs from nearby stone homes. Now the vineyards and olive trees emerged in the early daylight, a special treat reserved for those who were up at this hour. Ein Kerem was, indeed, true to its name, a fountain of light. Its dawn-like aura spilled over those who walked in its midst.

A tephilined, talised ancient oriental, whose white hair had turned yellow under his faded, colourless yarmulka, appeared. What at a distance had seemed a shadow of a stooped, bearded figure in slow motion, approached as a twinkly eyed, Yemenitesounding psalmster. Across the road a young, tall kafiyahed, dark-skinned man walked swiftly in the direction of a mosque from which came the call of the muezzin, A recalcitrant donkey was running away from a brown-hooded and robed Fraciscan monk who had attempted to remove a parcel from the animal's saddle. The bells of the Visitation Church, at the corner, chimed, and the brother seemed all the more intent on catching the beast. Out of nowhere leaped a large, black, barking dog, which could not resist chasing the poor ass, which occasionally reversed the sport by charging at the dog. A few kind souls from among those waiting at the bus stop, ready for another day of work, decided they had nothing immediately to do and joined the pursuit of the high strung hee-hawing rebel. A rooster, who had only shortly before announced the sunrise, felt compelled by the commotion to confirm that indeed, it was morning, a new day in Ein Kerem.

"LOOK OVER"

"LOOK OVER"

It was Shabbat and we were walking on the northeastern section of the wall of the Old City. He was leading me. He had been here before and wanted to share that which he could not, or perhaps would not attempt to, explain. As a matter of fact, he never explained very much. He was always quiet, often nodding, laughing when laughter was appropriate, parceling out his words, not for the purpose of showing that he was a good listener for a return of gratitude, but simply to give reassurance that he was considering what was being said.

When he responded or made a comment, it was well thought out, precise, to the point. Re-emphasis was not his style. Nothing was outwardly emphasized in him. He was fair, of average height, yet slight, very thin with a neatly trimmed full beard and wire-framed glasses. Everything about him seemed to fit; everything was there for a purpose. His economy with words was an extension of his being. A conversation could go on in which, after an hour, he might have phrased only two or three sentences; yet there was no doubt he had been engaged in a dialogue. He respected and wanted to hear all that was being said and I quickly learned to respect his silence as active participation.

We had met only a short while ago. Certainly it was his wise, gentle, quietude that drew me to him, more than that our professions, backgrounds, beliefs and interests were rather similar.

He had come to Jerusalem alone, leaving behind in New York, his mother, brothers, an advisory position, relative comfort. It was the first visit, made some five years before, that had decided it all. He had then spent his summers generally in Israel, particularly in Jerusalem, acclimatizing himself, preparing for his eventual emigration. Once, in an expansive moment, he said that the process had been perfectly natural, even if for those who had been in his midst it did not seem so. He now worked, in a role which combined his academic and professional backgrounds of legal training and urban planning, on environmental and quality-of-life projects in and for Jerusalem.

"Look," he said, pointing to bullet holes next to the Lion's gate (St. Stephen's gate, Shaar Ha'arayot). "During the Six Day War, Zahal, the Israel Army, could not bomb the area due to the government's policy of preserving the Holy Places of the three religions. Large numbers of soldiers, advancing from the Kidron Valley below, were held up here as Jordanians shot at them from the buildings and high terrain. It was at this spot that the Israeli forces entered the Old City on June 7, 1967."

We walked slowly and stood and gazed at the Kidron Valley and still further westward, where the Kidron ends and the Hinnom (Purgatory) Valley begins. The two merge in a dry, rocky hollow, which only occasionally reveals a withered, solitary tree. I was reminded of Jeremiah. "And they have built the high places of Topheth, which is in the valley of the son of Hinnom, to burn their sons and their daughters of the fire, which I commanded them not, neither came it into my heart. Therefore the day cometh, saith the Lord, that it shall not be called Topheth, not the valley of the son of Hinnom, but the valley of slaughter; for they shall bury in Topheth till there be no place. And the carcasses of the people shall be meat for the fowls of the heavens and for the beasts of the earth, and none shall frighten them away." (Jeremiah 7:31-33).

Making our way down and turning right along the eastern wall towards the Dung Gate, we approached a curve in the road and crossed a bridge spanning the Kidron Valley. We came to a pair of sculpted wings, one of which was broken, symbolizing the paratroopers who had given their lives here, and the other lifted as if for flight, symbolizing the victory the sacrifice had brought.

His green, reflective eyes, behind the delicate spectacles, viewed the horizon, following the line of the raised wing towards the Mount of Olives. This is the oldest and largest Jewish cemetery in the world, and it is believed that at the end of days the resurrection of the dead will occur in front of Mount Moriah, the Temple Mount which it faces. My mind went back to the broken wing and I recalled Zehariah's vision: "Behold the Day of the Lord cometh . . . and his feet shall stand in that day upon the Mount of Olives which is before Jerusalem . . . and men shall dwell thereto and there shall be no more extermination but Jerusalem shall dwell safely." (Zehariah 14:1-11).

Lifting our heads and looking further to the northeast, we saw Mount Scopus, to which he pointed, *Har Ha Zofim* which means to "look over."

A GRANDFATHER'S SIGNATURE AND HIS GRANDDAUGHTER'S PRAYER AT THE WALL

A GRANDFATHER'S SIGNATURE AND HIS GRANDDAUGHTER'S PRAYER AT THE WALL

He put a yarmulka on his grey-haired head. His hair had been grey for as long as I could remember. Slowly, after one more instant of reflection, he signed the release form with deliberation. There had been no hesitation in the pause. Rather, I was sure, he had been quickly reviewing his life up to this moment. His well known aristocratic family, gone, killed: his first wife, his son, his two sisters, his father, his mother, his famous uncle, his brothers-in-law, had all vanished along with just about everyone from his past. His present family: wife and two sons, one but a child of ten, the other older, but not yet of age to volunteer for civilian duty during the latest war in the history of his people. The decision, he knew, was preordained, like the duel he had offered as a student and won for the honour of his people, when a quota system was announced in pre-war Vienna; like his being wounded in the forests of Poland, where he had fought among the partisans; like his active, concrete service to the beleaguered Zionist State in post-war Paris. His going to the shores of the St. Lawrence, in a new country, which he always called blessed for its freedom, could not be otherwise. His expressive, sad blue-grey eyes looked up as he held out the paper. His signature on it was neat, distinctive, showing pride in the formation of the name. It was like his handshake, strong, complete, dignified, imparting his word, which to him, and in the teachings he gave his sons, was sacred.

Even sitting, he looked distinguishedly handsome. He was tall, always well groomed and well dressed. His concession to relaxation from frequent overwork was to loosen his tie and open his first shirt button. Somehow he always looked dignified without appearing to be formal when the situation did not warrant it. He always made others feel at ease in his company and related on whatever level suited them and the occasion. His complexion was fair, his upper cheeks often red because of high blood pressure. His pale colour worried me, but not enough.

While he was writing, I had noticed and admired his hands, as I always did. He did not believe in rings for men; he wore only his simple gold wedding band and a fine watch on his left hand. One was immediately drawn to his hands, because his firm handshake was a symbol of his character; yet they were delicate hands, pale, thin, finely proportioned, with veins predominant. They revealed the strength of his personality and its delicateness all at once.

As I looked at the newly reclaimed ancient Kotel (Western Wall), the scene of the signing flashed over and over again as if screened on the temple rocks. A shiver of fear came over me and I offered a prayer for my Father's health. I gathered a few loose pebbles from the wall which ultimately landed a few weeks later in his grave in Montreal under the tombstone bearing his proud name.

Mount Moriah, the Temple Mount upon which the first and second temples' layered wall stands, is said to be the place where Abraham intended to sacrifice his son before the hand of God stopped him. The word *mora,* awe, which combines fear and reverence, was contained for me in the most sacred Jerusalem dust, which I gathered as my father was gathered unto his people.

Ten years passed by. I tightly held her tiny delicate hand in my hand, yet made sure that my grasp would not hurt her. Her brown soft curls adorned her finely textured face, dominated by expressive blue-grey eyes. She looked at the Kotel and at the people; and then at a little bird in flight descending and ascending and said, "Papa, Papa, look at the *Zippor Katana*. He looks so free, he can do whatever he likes. No one is stopping him; he flies wherever and whenever he wants. Can people go where they want, when they want, just like the bird? Papa, can I say a prayer like everyone else here? Please, Papa, I only have one, that everyone be like that bird.''

Sometime later, I discovered that in the vicinity of the southern wall of the temple where a child's prayer had been heard, a large stone bears the words of Isaiah's prophecy: ''And when you see this, your heart shall rejoice, and your bones shall flourish like young grass.'' (Isaiah 66:14).

A CHARCOAL ETCHING
BURSTS INTO FLAME

A CHARCOAL ETCHING BURSTS INTO FLAME

I was one of three outwardly non-Hassidic-looking men praying in their shtibl on Friday evenings. The small synagogue was housed in a tiny decrepit building with plaster falling from what appeared to have been, at one time, white-washed ceilings and walls, and portions of windows boarded up where they had been broken. As the Kabbalat Shabbat service began, the Jerusalem sun, setting on the hills and valleys, entered through the remaining apertures, giving the room, with its plain wooden chairs, stools and occasional long tables, a prismatic aura. The deep blue velvet Ark curtains with crimson and gold letters and symbols of the twelve tribes, which only a few minutes ago had provided the only color, now gave their hues to every corner of the room. Prior to the chanting of the psalms, the room had had the character of a black and white etching, produced by the traditional dress of the Hassidim—the black satin robe and gartel (belt), white tieless shirt and black shtreimel—and even by the beards and earlocks which were predominantly black and white.

The exuberant Hassidic welcome given the Shabbat bride in their fervent niggunum (melodies) seemed to transport the very structure into a roaring flame both for reason of its fervency and the deepening colors, which had by now inundated the place.

He sat there, surrounded everywhere by tall folio volumes in a small study, as in an oil painting. His brown eyes intense, penetrating, wise, kindly and burning. Somehow those eyes, which were all of these, also appeared tired, yet resigned to the inevitable fatigue. They reflected the constant parade of those who came in want of blessing, judgment, compassion, discernment, or just the comfort of being in his midst, which went on and on. The skin of his hands and face was translucent; it seemed the epitome of cleanliness. Its paleness, which had a yellow tint due to inadequate exposure to direct sunlight, took on the hues of anything near or encompassing him, as a crystal picks up adjacent lights. Although he was dressed in black, with greying beard and earlocks, the contrasts in colors, the effects of light and shadow on him were as the distinctions among both in the words of the havdalah prayer at the completion of the Sabbath.

Entranced by the rhythm of the chant, I did not at first hear the translucent Rebbe calling to me, *Mein Kind,* my child, in a warm caring tone. This slight, thin man completely filled the scene with his serenity. From a land two oceans away, a direct descendant of the Baal Shem Tov, holding court in the only diaspora self-contained shtetl of Chagalesque perception, surrounded by towns bearing French-Canadian names, appeared.

The Rebbe's penetrating eyes, the wisdom of the large folio volumes, the Kabbalat Shabbat, the niggunum and the lights of the Hassidim accompanied me with color on my walk through Meah Shearim; without them the scene would have been a monochrome. A series of streets in which the attached row-houses, synagogues and yeshivas were built in rectangular fashion, one hundred and five years ago, with windows and doors in an inner courtyard, unknown to those who see its fortress-like exterior. Closed off from the outside world for the purpose of defense and preservation of its way of life, this community had changed little in its century of existence. Eternity or a striving for it has no variation. The six hundred and thirteen commandments to which the Hassidim adhere have yet to be amended. What they would have gained, if anything, by alteration is a matter of opinion.

According to Rav Kuk, the first chief rabbi of Israel, who explained the concept of "Ahavat Israel," love of each member of the community is a prerequisite, not a matter of opinion.

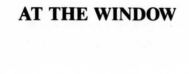

AT THE WINDOW

AT THE WINDOW

He stood alone at the window. It was Friday afternoon. The building was empty. No one would know that he was there except the guard and I. His door was open; his office, large by Israeli standards, contained much furniture, yet without appearing to be cluttered. A large, stained dark brown table and hardwood chairs suggested a boardroom. Book-lined armoire shelves with windowed, wood framed doors bordered the table at its long sides. A space separated the table, where he sat in a moved-in chair, when he presided at meetings, from his desk, which hinted of dark wood under the neatly gathered opinion papers, case books, jurisprudence texts, memoranda, the official legal gazette and the overflowing in and out baskets. Two square black telephones rested on a metal table on the left of his desk chair. A large quilted tapestry made by his artist wife represented a bus, aeroplane, train and ship, all leaving from the same point, traveling toward answers in the various legal reference texts in the room. The once whitewashed walls, although clean, had turned yellow with age.

A solitary, tall figure, he faced away from me, so that I saw the back of his dark, faded, well pressed suit, of which the jacket appeared considerably shorter in back than in front. The long, thin, pale hands appeared to dangle alongside his slight long frame. His thin, yet full head of grey hair was neatly in place, meeting the black glass frames at the well proportioned ears, and continued a short way down the long, white neck which ended at the greying white shirt collar. I noticed that his pants were too short, revealing grey socks entering black, worn, but polished shoes whose scuff marks were too deeply ingrained to be shined out.

I had never seen him so still for so long, or so it seemed that instant. The tiny antechamber, which held his two secretaries and in which I stood, reverberated with the rattle of typewriters and the ringing of telephones. The secretaries' voices were hushed as if in fear of disturbing him. They would be finishing work which he might have needed yesterday, or urgently putting it aside so that a new priority item, whether involving a shipping strike or a transportation link would be ready for a Knesset committee hearing. Only at such times or when he was not in the office, would they and others of his subordinates temper their restraint and allow the sounds of their exuberance to be heard. A sigh of relaxation would sweep the halls from his end of the second floor to the other, which housed a small library, in which the newest and most junior incumbents shared space at four desks in the ceiling-to-floor book-filled room.

From his window on Ibn Gabirol Street, in the building which had served as the Office of the Prime Minister at the creation of the State, in this highest part of tranquil residential Rehavia, an open field allowed him to gaze directly on King George Street opposite the Jewish Agency structure. In front of this building further on, he could see the offices of the World Zionist Organization, the Keren Hayesod and the Keren Kayemet Le Israel, and beyond, the rainbow-flowered, green-treed, sloping gardens of the municipality. The chalk-grey Old City with its barren rock walls, the tower of David and the Mount of Olives provided a top for the three dimensional frame which bordered his vision with a dab of clear blue sky, darkened by hues of the mountains of Transjordan (Moab and Gilead) in the distance.

I knocked, hesitant to disturb him, however unwilling not to, as I did not want to leave without his knowledge that someone had indeed intruded on his private moment. As he turned from the window, I apologized and wished him Shabbat Shalom. He beckoned me in.

The tense face, to which I had become accustomed, was now relaxed. The phone calls, the voices of others, still sounded in the halls. His authority and competence were so firmly established that he could put aside his usual hurried, purposeful manner and stern expression for my unexpected visit. I noticed that his blue-grey eyes behind black-rimmed glasses looked exhausted. Although deeply lined, his face was tightly drawn; nothing sagged. He faced again to the window and talked to me all at once; I was there but he felt as comfortable with me as if I was not. I was grateful that indeed I had not interrupted him.

If he had not interspersed his words every so often with "you know," I would not have thought that he was speaking to me. He was and he was not. I felt sorry that the calm with which his presence filled the room was not known by those working in his midst, six days a week, some for as long as he had held his position—thirty years—they thinking of his retirement, he never hinting at it.

"Within two months, both my sons will be in the army." The eldest had served the first year of a three year enlistment and the younger one must now begin his period of duty.

"The constant threats of all our neighbors, the hidden mines, the terrorist bombs, the border incursions..."

As to the life expectancy of his sons, not much had changed since he had come to this country. Their chances hung in the same balance. His heavy words weighed upon the setting of the sun, the fast approaching Shabbat, and the fragrant air I was anticipating on my walk home.

My youth provoked a sorrowful, compassionate laugh. "No, you who are filled with enthusiasm—it is hard to understand. After years, faces, friends, employees, so many, suddenly, gone, and over and over again, year after year. As if reviewing a procession, he slowly enunciated each word. "Their stubborn, determined spirit, unbroken, haughty, insolent, lax, egocentric, selfish youth turned into obedient, disciplined, overworked, caring, responsible, selfless, ageless heroes, some of whom will never have the opportunity to grow old.''

He turned towards the window, looking far into the distance beyond the Transjordanian Mountains. ''They will now both serve.''

WE HAD TURNED THE CORNER

WE HAD TURNED THE CORNER

We had turned the corner at King George Street and were standing on Gaza Road. A whistling breeze swept through the closely knit cypress, feather-like willow, and solitary palm trees shading Rehavia stirring up a fragrant flower, leaf and grass scent. A mother pushed her umbrella stroller; and a young man emerged from a flower shop with a white paper wrapped bouquet tied with a pink ribbon. The schoolyard on the opposite side of Ibn Gabirol Street (named after the lonely scholar who is said to have sung God's praises as sweetly as a nightingale and whose songs echo throughout the ages from his short life in 11th century Spain to the prayerbook of the Day of Atonement), which we had just passed, was noticeably empty. The children who played there throughout the day, the entire summer, were in their classrooms, waiting for the final afternoon school bell to ring. The suburb, known as "God's expanse," with streets named for lyrical poets, mystic philosophers and legalistic thinkers of the Middle Ages, seemed to reverberate in its stillness with solely our conversation.

"What will I tell my sons if the wars continue, if we have the chance for peace and do not take it? But do we know that this is peace? What risks must we take? How great can the risks be? Can the risks, can peace prove disastrous, a point of no return? Will we seize the opportunity? Can we seize the opportunity? What if we miss it? But how will I tell them that we tried? Will we, and then did we? When my sons leave in their uniforms, will I be able to answer their questions?"

One question after another, it seemed as if there was no end, and then a long silence. The rapid staccato of questions came out of nowhere, and yet as if from everywhere. He abruptly stopped my first inquiry as to whether the negotiating team, of which he was a member, felt that the shipping strike was almost over. There was something more important on his mind as he put it; all else was secondary.

"Where will the talks with Sadat lead? What must be given to him, what risks for peace? Yes, this generation must take all the risks. What a dilemma. To be faced with dangers was one thing. One was at least at peace with oneself. But now choices are required. Will we make the right ones?"

Then there were no more questions, not a word. He was no longer with me. Only his tall, heavy frame, short curly brown hair, blue laughing eyes, which often became moist, large, pudgy reddish face, thick neck, navy blazer, too short and too tight, grey pants which had long been outgrown, were present. It was the body of a big man with a child's expression of desire for reassurance on his face. This large, cuddly, teddy bear seemed to want so much to be told that all would simply work out well, to be comforted. One would never have believed that he was old enough to have fought in the last two wars.

Within an instant, we had travelled up Mount Scopus; and he was now observing his sons in his apartment in Ramat Eshkol, a district of the virtually treeless sector reclaimed in 1967. His younger son, now nine years old, thin like his wife, curly haired like him, freckles inherited from heaven knows whom, couldn't wait to get out to play soccer, climb trees, shout and engage in mischievous pranks. What a chore to make him look at a book! It was as if he was allergic to school and the indoors, a child of the streets. His brother, a year older, straight haired, brown eyed and wearing glasses like his mother, had a roundish build and was shorter than the younger. From the moment the older boy had been able to reach the keys of the piano, it seemed he could play it. Once he began lessons, he and his piano were as one. His somewhat chubby fingers conducted a daily three-to-four hour dialogue on the keyboard. His renowned teacher often spoke of "the child's deep rooted sensitivity," as if his father and mother needed to be told. The neighbors had already decided that the lad would be a concert pianist and that the disturbances were a necessary sacrifice, for his practicing continued from just about his return from school until his bedtime, interrupted only by mealtimes and the inevitable fight with his brother, which ended with both parents screaming. Although heaven help whoever else dared tease or hurt him: his younger brother considered it a matter of personal pride to protect his special older sibling. As far as homework was concerned, he spent all of twenty minutes, between his scales to do it, receiving blue stars which he did not bother to show his parents. Had they not examined his exercise books, only his report cards and parent-teacher meetings would have informed them of his progress. His school teacher described him as "a born mathematician with a flare for poetry, a joy to teach, far ahead of his class." Just as his brother could not be coaxed or threatened to come in, he could not be to go out.

When they put on their military uniforms, how will I answer them?

YESTERDAY—NINETEEN YEARS BEFORE

YESTERDAY—NINETEEN YEARS BEFORE

"And Rabbi Akiba wanted so much to give his wife the world and more, her devotion, love, admiration and respect knew no borders. She eked out a living for them both so that he could learn and reach his full potential, and thus greatness, which as it turned out was not only for him but an influential source of strength, which endured even the unsuccessful revolt against the Romans in 132 B.C.E. He may have been martyred but his undaunted spirit, symbolizing preservation by study, lives on.

"Rabbi Akiba has also left us a self-portrait of Jerusalem. As he had only started to study at the age of forty, he felt his wife had missed much; although she felt she had gained all. Akiba told her that he wished he could buy her a symbol of his love, a golden Jerusalem, a medallion with an impression of the landmarks of the city. Just as the Jerusalem sunset transforms the city with its golden hues, reflecting from its mountains, hills, and barren rocks, so would her medallion be transforming. After a few years, Rachel received her Jerusalem from Akiba; and we receive sun-kissed Jerusalem, as if tucked in a golden blanket, before it falls asleep to awaken to yet another day."

The master storyteller had told one more story, one more time. It may have been for the thousandth or two thousandth time or more. It was as if Rabbi Akiba was a neighbor who had finally realized his promise, and the eighteen hundred and fifty years between then and now had disappeared.

The recounter of tales was sitting in his tree-surrounded Jerusalem living room on Radak Street, surrounded by two rabbis, a nun, a priest, professors of various faiths, tourists, neighbors, students, his two sons—one a hero commander of daring missions, the other an engineering professor—and, of course, his wife. She was an aristocratic, Sorbonne-educated, grey haired lady, his devoted companion, friend and admirer. Although she had heard the story many times, her full attention was directed toward him; and when he turned to her, because he looked at each person as he related the tale, it was with the silently enquiring glance of a newlywed. *Was it not so, Ester?* And she nodded approvingly.

His booming voice resounded with enthusiasm from his broad-shouldered, robust, big, strong body. The laughing eyes, full head of thick grey-white hair, broad smile as amiable as the bear hug he had given each of us upon greeting. No wonder he was called the pied piper.

"Ah," he said, "did you know that there is background music to my story, now your story. Yerushalayim Shel Zahav (Jerusalem of Gold), the song of the Six Day War, as it was called, although Naomi Shemer sang it just prior to the restoration of the unity of the city. That was during the tension filled weeks, culminating in Hussein's call to his subjects to join Nasser's Holy War."

He paused somewhere in the midst of a scene in a story, which perhaps we later heard or read, or perhaps, was only his. Quietly, he said, "But please, I want to hear you." Everyone spontaneously beckoned him on. *Please continue.*

A lullabye, in Polish traveled from France and Canada to a grown man, sitting, listening, wanting to hear more. And the words reverberated clearly in my ears. *Move Dalei, Move Dalei, Move Yesche.* Speak further. Speak further, tell more enchanting stories, tales of awe. My mother's soft words were interrupted by a voice belonging to a tall, blond, bespectacled professor of religion, who called out in his midwestern American accent, "In 1948, how was Mount Zion penetrated?"

Then in rapid fire, our host told of how as operations officer on active duty during the War of Independence, he had proposed that a tunnel be dug from the Mishkenot Shaananim buildings at Yemin Moshe to Shaama in the Hinnom Valley, allowing soldiers to approach at the foot of Mount Zion. A three pronged attack was carried out. "New Gate was entered by an I.Z.L. force, a L.H.Y. group entered near Jaffa Gate, and Zion Gate was penetrated by a Haganah unit."

While coffee was being served, an archeologist with a British accent told me that he had heard our host thirty years ago, in a group of three thousand people who were touring the walls of the Old City. "To this day, I can see Nehemia of twenty-five hundred years ago rebuilding the city walls, through his words describing the scene as a three-dimensional painting with the sounds and scents of the time. He gave me history, in layers, removing them gently not to do harm. I felt as if I was on an archeological dig at a tel, separating the ages, giving life to the inhabitants, and imbuing the present settlers with past purposes and future hopes. He taught me to look at a place here and beyond. I feel as if I can see it, not once, but two or three, or even more times, with so much more to discover each time, witnessing past events on soil which was forming—different casts with different props but always on the same set. Soon the whole country seemed an extension of this city. It was as if he had walked each inch of its territory, old, new and again reclaimed, from the age of twelve when he was told, *Ya Beni, my son,* by a Bedouin, *if you are afraid, go back to your mother's dress.*

A tribute on his seventieth birthday from the land and people provided the background to my thoughts even as I listened. "For seventy years he did not stop walking by himself and guiding others: from the time he led the weekly field trips as a student at the Teachers Seminary in Jerusalem, where the geography teacher asked him to guide his fellow classmates, to giving lectures for the Histadrut (General Federation of Labour) Cultural Committee

during the 'era of the roads' of the twenties, when the Third
Aliya (Immigration) was breaking stones with hammers and chis-
els to build roads, to the era of the new settlements, where he
would describe the flora, fauna and rocks within their historical
geographical setting, inviting the personalities from the Bible,
Talmud, Middle Ages to the present from his address book,
thumbed at will, and introducing them to their new neighbours
with whom they now shared the same space. This Yediat
Ha'aretz, Knowledge of the Country, he gave to all who came in
contact with him, whether through more than thirty published
books, or personally to students in the military academy or walking tourists—and just about every native inhabitant was a tourist
with him. As one walker in a uniform with wings amongst a few
thousand told him, 'I know every important landmark in Cairo
but I didn't know Jerusalem.' And after the Six Day War, he
went with army units to point out every corner of the Old City,
which he had walked yesterday, nineteen years before.''

As the late summer afternoon's first story was casting its gold-
en shadows into the room and on his face, his wife announced
that perhaps he was a little tired. He concluded, ''Every tale
shows we suffered much but we never lost hope. The key to Jerusalem, to the country, to my story is hope.''

As we walked down the stairs from his apartment, a young
self-assured Israeli, hardened by the Yom Kippur War, who had
met him for the first time, exclaimed, ''Only after knowing that
he participated in four wars, do I understand that the word naivete is a cynical translation of hope. However which dictionary will
show that?''

I heard from someone who had recently seen him that his wife
is no longer with him, but that he had said she had left the golden
medallion, Yerushalayim Shel Zahav, which he had given her, for
him to keep.

JERUSALEM BREEZES

JERUSALEM BREEZES

He lay there, several layers of white, thin gauze bandage over his eyes. By the time I arrived, his sister-in-law had told me he would certainly be blind in one eye and that the other eye might have been saved, but this was not yet certain. His wife was simply not there. Perhaps the strain was too much for her and she had escaped. She returned at intervals. His parents, from Rishon Le Zion, came as often as they could. The trauma of this event provoked a heart attack in his father, who had lost his entire first family in Auschwitz.

The plastic surgeon came in to examine the badly burnt face, which at an earlier stage could not be bandaged. Its ravaged left side had had to dry as much as possible, after months of treatment, during which no one could enter his breathing space lest he be infected. He was enclosed in a plastic tent with wires leading to electrodes, connected to machines, so that continuous health newscasts could be instantly communicated while life was fed to him intravenously.

The young, white clad doctor, whose pale face and tired eyes betrayed the smile he showed to those in the room, examined the face in one quick look and told the patient whose black hair was shaved just above the ears, that within two or three days the bandages would be removed. Then he would know whether his right eye would give him sight. The thin, drawn physician then walked toward the window and said, "For God's sake, have this window opened. Just because you cannot see Mount Scopus and the surrounding view of Jerusalem from your room, does not mean that you should not feel Jerusalem with its breezes. And it would certainly not hurt you, or for that matter your neighbor Hayim in the next bed, to have a little more noise in here. I should bring the nursery ward here to liven you fellows up, or better still, the oohing and ahing grandparents who surround the new-borns and tell us what we should do.''

A chuckle came from the next bed. ''You know, Doctor, you are really something. I came here for a vacation from my wife, four boys and three girls, one a baby, and you tell me I am missing noise.''

The doctor spoke to the nurse who had entered the room. ''You know, when I look at Hayim I ask myself, 'Why is he here?''

Strong looking, brown eyed, thick-necked, about forty years of age, big, bearded Hayim, who looked like a man of average height with a heavy set frame under the white sheet and blue blanket, answered: ''To keep an eye on things until Ami will, when you remove his bandages.''

Then he turned to his neighbor. ''Listen Ami, enough of this, I want to get some sleep. How much sleep do you think I get at home, with my wife giving me a daily running account of inflation? By the end of the day, I can give you the up-to-the-minute prices of everything, from chickens to sunflower seeds—all those figures! When my children, all under twelve, call me it's a relief. I still have a few years to enjoy before they realize that my fruit and vegetable store has not made me a millionaire. But who cares? For the meantime, they think we are very wealthy. I keep telling them that their mother is going to be Minister of Finance one day and that we will have a very prosperous country. Not that the children think they can buy everything. They have known otherwise for a long time. But they think because there are so many of them, nothing more would fit in our three bedroom apartment. And am I to tell them otherwise? I have not had one economic forecast for the three months, one week and three and one-half days I have been here. All I know is that when my wife visits me on Shabbat, when she is not minding the store, she has nothing but praise. She says that everything is provided for, thank God. You know, Doctor, I must say that even though I don't look forward to hearing her auditor's reports, I wouldn't mind going back to her, to my children. It's been a long time, Doctor. So listen, Ami. Enough of sleeping on the job—another couple of days of this and my eyes go on strike."

Ami's scorched face drew into a smile and he turned his head in the direction of the doctor and said, "Doctor, you better not disappoint Hayim."

There was a brief silence and the doctor responded quietly, "I will try not to." And he went out of the room.

I sat there, talking to Ami for a while, played checkers with Hayim, moving his men according to his instructions, gave Ami a glass of orange juice, which he knew where to place when he was finished, and I put a chocolate in Hayim's mouth, as both his hands were in casts. As I thought that perhaps both men could use some rest before supper, I bade them goodbye, promising to return the next day.

Walking down the hall, I saw a blond, freckled woman, in her early twenties, who cried softly, telling the orderly wheeling her bed that it was her first baby. An oriental father in oil-stained blue shirt and jeans looked as if he had not completely filled the last tank with gas. A whimpering cry of an older man came a few rooms away from the elevator, which I was approaching.

I thought about Ami and Hayim recalling Ami's sister-in-law's words. "All we know was that he left the university, arrived at the usual time for his part time work at the airport. This was the first luggage check of the afternoon. Two girls, who had just arrived from Cyprus with Dutch passports, told Ami they were in a hurry as they were certain family members were waiting for them, since their plane had been late. Ami apologized, but for some reason he felt he had to examine their baggage carefully. They sat down in the distance on the floor, hippie style, as if to talk. Ami noticed a transistor radio which his helper was about to take out. Suddenly Ami jumped, covered the suitcase with his body after slamming it shut, thus preventing the imminent explosion from causing more injuries and fatalities then it did. The casualty count was three dead, four seriously injured. One hundred and fifty people in the same room were unharmed. The ballistics expert estimated that Ami had saved the lives of at least forty-five people and prevented another twenty from sustaining injuries.''

After a pause, she said, "Ami always wanted to live in Jerusalem, to teach geography while showing his students Jerusalem, which would be his classroom. Now all he is waiting for is to be able to see it."

I had asked her on my first visit if she knew what had happened to Hayim.

"In 1967, Hayim was part of the force which reopened the very road to this hospital and to the University. The road was cut off from Jerusalem after it became part of Jordanian territory, although the buildings were guarded since the creation of the State by an alternating bi-weekly Israel Police Contingent under the supervision of U.N. observers. Apparently, Hayim found it most significant that the grave of Rabbi Simon Hazaddik was near that road. Hayim hoped that the words of this great, just sage, who was among the last of the survivors of the Great Assembly, to whom it is said that Alexander the Great bowed in humility, would one day be acclaimed: 'The world is based upon three principles: Torah, worship and kindliness.'

"During the Yom Kippur War, five men with whom he fought in tanks in the Sinai were killed by a mine. It was the last day of the war. He was the sole survivor after being in a coma for seven days, and to this day he cannot recall what happened. Now, five years later, he was to take his twelve year old son to a soccer game at the child's school. He had promised to go to the game if his son's class won the semi-final championships in his age group, which it did. He took the morning off from work, asked Tova to take care of the store, something he never did except when on

Miluim, reserve duty. In the school yard prior to the game, he found a suspicious brown package near a small shack used for sports equipment. The children were approaching the shed, as their school T-shirts for the soccer game were kept there. Hayim picked up the package and ran with it to a remote corner of the field. But he did not succeed in his purpose. The package erupted and threw him into the air. He never saw the soccer game. The children never played that day.

THEM, US AND WE IN JERUSALEM

THEM, US AND WE IN JERUSALEM

He was standing with his brown-eyed, long-dark-haired daughter, waiting for me. We had arranged to meet in front of the university's administrative offices. He was wearing brown sandals with two shiny buckles and double straps securing his ankles and toes. His grey, loose jacket revealed a white shirt open at the collar, and his pressed, flapping charcoal pants met his pale ankles at the distinctly Israeli-made Nimrod sandals on Jerusalem soil.

The southward-stretching, mountainous Givat Ram Campus (Kiryat-Ha-Universita), across from Hakirya, the Government Center buildings and the Knesset, housed its academic departments in a series of low circular or rectangular streamlined structures built on a ridge of the Judean Hills in the west of the City. At the entrance, a Henry Moore statue beckons students to approach.

Boris was pointing out the campus to his daughter. I greeted them and asked him to continue. He went on relating the history of the university to Katerina: "This campus was erected when Mount Scopus became inaccessible to professors and students in April of 1948, after a convoy of Jewish doctors, nurses and students were murdered. The former Hadassah Hospital, medical center and various departments had become famous from their inception in 1923. It was then that Albert Einstein delivered his first lecture on the theory of relativity there. He spoke the first few sentences in Hebrew, which was to become the teaching language."

"But Father, who decided to build a university here, and then?"

Boris continued, "Weitzman, then a professor at the University of Geneva, (through Herman Shapira's inspirational initiative as early as 1884), and Martin Buber proclaimed that the modern foundation of nationhood must begin in academies. But it was Herzl who submitted a petition to the Ottoman Sultan to establish the university after the Zionist Congress of 1901."

Boris was a born educator, despite his origins, a respected principal in Moscow for five years and a mathematics teacher for fifteen years. It was only when he applied for an exit visa five years ago that the textbooks he had written were removed from the curriculum; and for this he was obliged to tutor privately. Not a difficult fate, as he put it. His brother was denied the right to emigrate and refused permission to stay on as chief pediatrician in the hospital in which he had worked for twenty-three years. Now he was accompanying his daughter to her medical school admissions interview, telling her how he wished he had started his career here. They had between them two immediate goals: her acceptance into medical school so that she might pursue the profession she had witnessed her mother practice for as long as she could remember, and his learning to speak Hebrew fluently enough to teach in a classroom again. His accounting position was too divorced from the teaching of students, he had grown to love, and which had been denied him ever since his teaching staff in the Soviet Union had discovered and reported that he was studying the Hebrew language to the district supervisor of schools. Boris was duly informed, within hours, that the language of Zionists did not mix with the proper upbringing and cherished education of Soviet youth.

It was almost three o'clock; Boris and I told Katerina that we would wait for her at the amphitheater, beyond the planetarium and the student center, as we had pointed out to her on the campus map.

On the way to the amphitheater, I noticed the tent-like white circular synagogue, typical of crafted structures from the desert, which could be approached from all directions.

Boris and I sat down without exchanging one word: he an anxious father awaiting his daughter's return and I simply a friend with whom he wanted to spend some time. The empty amphitheater encased us in blue sky and streaming sunshine. I was not able to see the performance going on in Boris' mind, but images from his former world, which I had briefly viewed as an outsider a millenium ago, flashed in mine. Somehow the two worlds met here because of his presence and mine and our reunion in Jerusalem. Whereas his former colleagues had cast him aside because he studied Hebrew, we had become friends for the very same reason.

Every tree, bush and uneven blade of grass came back to me. Lenin's eyes were staring from every corner of the park. His stone profile turned continually in my direction. It was as if I was standing still and he was moving everywhere. God, I walked and walked for four days, telling whoever I could find that we did care, that they must know, that they must not give up hope. Yes, I admitted, the numbers were not large, the names few in comparison with total populations, but there were those who cherished the hope and nurtured the prayer for that day. Yes, it was true we hoped and they struggled. We spoke and they were silenced. We were questioning our consciences and they were being interrogated. And then I met this roly poly man, short, bald except for a fringe of white short-cropped hair above the neck. Between inhaling his cigaretts, he choked and coughed: "I am sorry that there is no synagogue available to which you can go. All prayer in Lvov is in private minyans." and as he bade me goodbye he said, "I beg you, for your own good, do not pray with us, do not raise your voice in our presence. Raise your voice where it counts."

Rain pounded the grey pavement. The grey sky enveloped the grey buildings and swallowed the grey Dnieper River. It seemed as if everything was melting, but it was not. The greyness turned to night. I arrived at the synagogue, after a bus ride through winding streets, to be greeted at the door by a dark grey silhouette in a wide-brimmed hat and long coat. I was ushered immediately to a seat isolated from the few other silhouettes in the darkened synagogue by a low, solid, dark panel. More shadows arrived for the Mariv (evening prayers). I nodded my greeting, still sitting in my separate seat. But after the Borchu (the beginning of the evening service), I stood up, pushed aside the panel, walked down the ten rows towards the front benches of the middle section, which faced the *Ner Tamid* (the Eternal Light), stopped abruptly and took a seat in the third row. The capped silhouette next to me was reciting the Shema. The grey silhouette in the wide-brimmed hat approached me indicating that he had pointed out my seat. I pointed to the Ark, signalling that I wanted to be closer, and did not want to be alone. I opened my arms as if to say it is good to pray together and loudly began chanting the Shema for all to hear. The capped silhouette moved away from me as if wanting to make the greatest distance between us possible. I knew I must speak to him. And if I did, it would have to be here and now, for I had been told that the silence of Kiev is impenetrable.

I finished my Shema, attempted a niggun in broken Yiddish. "Do you know we are? Please tell me how you are? How are the Jews of Kiev?"

The capped silhouette at first did not answer; then he groaned. "Please go. Don't endanger us more. Life is difficult enough."

I continued praying, looking towards the Ark, the Eternal Light. A voice came from underneath the cap. In the same whisper in which he had been praying, he said, "Yes! Whoever comes must know, you must know, whoever will listen to you when you are gone must know. Just tell them we are, and ask them if they are. Please. They must make their cries heard. We cannot." He walked out with me into the pelting night. The Ner Tamid was inside.

At sunrise, I was back for the Shahrit (Morning Service). The wide-brimmed, grey-coated moving figure with lifted collar pointed out to me my assigned, now particularly reserved, seat, which he told me as a guest of honor I could not decline. I did not. However, before I sat down, an ancient pale-faced, white-bearded, navy-blue-capped white haired head on a small thin body covered in dark wool appeared. This Chagall marionette shuffled down the aisle like those plastic toys whose feet and legs descend an incline by the force of gravity. He looked at me with dancing eyes, greeted me with a *Shalom Aleihem* and chuckled: "Tell him," he told the usher. "Make an old man happy or I will tell him who I am. I was Sholom Aleichem's driver. I drove the *ferdelah*. I commanded them: *Ferdelah fur*. Move, horsies, move." Suddenly my laughter cut through yesterday's silence and my obedience to sit where I was told. Speech could be ordered but I had burst into laughter; and my laughter had shattered the silence, if for but a moment.

I looked at Boris, gently slapped him on the back; and said, *"Yi ye ba seder* (it will work out just fine)." I stopped. I knew he would be preoccupied until Katerina came back. I looked at my watch. She had been at her exam for only fifteen minutes; for Boris it must have been much longer.

He turned to me and said, "She will be a great physician."

"I know," I replied.

And he, without listening, went on, "She will never have to leave." He looked down at the empty stage to whatever scene made up his set.

I was walking near the Hermitage, in the Baltic port city that was born as a Russian window to the west, along the Neva River, towards the benches to which Yitshak had given me directions in the synagogue. A tall, dark handsome fellow, he had simply said, "I will be there later for sure." Later I understood that to mean, even if others are not. There had been five Hebrew-speaking girls and seven boys; if there were more, I cannot remember. I recall only that they all spoke Hebrew.

We walked on and on in circles, crossing bridge after bridge, passing palatial buildings. It was as if we were drinking invisible coffee in a cafe outside of reality, exchanging stories as if he was no longer there but somewhere else. And every so often we awoke in our imaginary bistro and I told him, "You are in great danger." Once, twice, twenty times, I repeated the warning. For hours we walked without cease.

He said: "I must speak to brothers, must breathe freedom, and I can only breathe it in your presence because you have it and it is contagious." I exhorted, begged, reminded him, as if he needed to be reminded that his grandmother had died for her desire to emigrate revealed during an interrogation which had held one question too many. After five hours together, we parted at the hospital where he was on call, and a year later I met him in an operating room a few miles from this amphitheater and half a mile from the Hadassah Hospital, where Alexander, his sabra was born.

Katerina walked towards us, a shy reticent smile acknowledging my presence, but inwardly bursting with exuberance. We laughed. We knew how her exam had gone.

REDEMPTION

REDEMPTION

I was returning to Jerusalem, and they were accompanying me, victims and survivors, those whom I could name and see and the invisible six million whom I could not. The Egged bus climbed the Judean Hills, gradual slopes and jagged peaks of varying shades of grey, brown and white rock which glistened in the afternoon sun. The highway was marked with rusty, blood-red frames of tanks, half tracks and trucks which had burst into flame during the battles of the War of Independence, now testimonials to the convoys which had relieved the siege of Jerusalem.

The blue explosion of the Mediterranean Sea, which I had left less than two hours ago, had merged with the vapory blue sky at the foot of the mountain cemetery outside of Haifa. DR. SHMUEL GOLDMAN was engraved on the tombstone, unveiled for the wind-swept gathering of eyes which took in the sea, the sky, the mountain, the southward highway and the stone in a single panorama.

A gently wrinkled, heavy framed, yet thin, grey haired, bespectacled man in a blue trench coat and beret spoke as if conveying the final judgement of a court much higher than one from which he had recently retired. "Our gentle, quiet, modest, smiling, small, big friend, Dr. Shmuel Goldman died for a third time. First, in Auschwitz, where his wife and daughter were killed, then at the end of the war, when he discovered that most of his family had been murdered, and here again. But between the first two times and now, although he always lived with the memories of his beloved ones, he was redeemed and he redeemed. Upon his liberation from the concentration camp, he determined to settle and practice medicine in Israel. It was his sole purpose in life. There could be no other for him. His second companion in life understood his past and realized it would forever be part of his present. She accepted that. His only future, and he believed in the future, was Israel. However, he refused to be consumed by the Holocaust. His message was one of optimism. Although a major part of his life had ended in crematoria, he believed that Jewish history did not. He would not concede to Hitler this victory. For him the State of Israel meant redemption. Have we learned from him? But more important have we, his friends, taught that to our children? Will they, as the future generation of leaders, be able to follow through on the message of his life? I leave the grave of our dear friend who traveled from Poland to Israel with a stop in hell and still retained his dignity, tranquil nature and ceaseless, compassionate patience toward others. Dr. Goldman was indeed true to his name, a golden man.''

On a hill in western Jerusalem, ashes of victims from Auschwitz and other camps brought to Yad Vashem repose in a low building with a top layer of cement and a lower layer of embedded rocks. Guarded outside by tall, majestic trees it is a fortress dedicated to the preservation of memories of extinguished European Jewry. In one darkened room, one flame quivers for each annihilation camp; in another, a list of as many names of the perished as can be assembled grows. In a third, a museum of pictures, exhibits and words of personal recollection surrounds the observers. There is also a library, among whose books is the Institute's prize-winning *Matzevot* by Dr. Jakub Herzig. Therein "each word spoken here, anywhere and everywhere on behalf of the martyrs" is described "as the only way by which to attempt to give each victim a tombstone."

Cinders from burnt offerings, the sea-swept mountain wind, and the approaching desert breezes from Jerusalem mixed in the fast moving bus to focus my mind on monuments or the lack of them, which I had traveled seven years ago to witness in an endless unveiling.

The solid, red brick, empty fortress-like buildings surrounded by a fence with the *Arbeit Macht Frei* slogan on top of its entrance gate, seemed to deny nature's right to grow hardy grass, tall trees and colorful flowers, or even for the sun to shine there; but it did. The stench of the gas chambers had not precluded the regenerative process of life from occurring even at Auswitz.

Large, small, brown, black, grey, worn, new, torn, resewn shoes were stacked floor to ceiling in a warehouse room in every size. But no prince had searched far and wide to discover to which orphaned Cinderella each pair belonged. Here the shoes remained, their owners' identity long since forgotten. Another gymnasium-sized room held caps upon caps, for heads of every conceivable shape, clustered like pebbles on a beach. In the next room spectacles of an infinite variety of prescription, bore witness to the fact that eye-sight was no longer needed where their owners had gone.

And the brown wooden structures of Majdanek's wholesale warehouses contained the remnants of the most complete inventory ever assembled of man's inhumanity to man . . .

It was not a house, not a street, not a number. *"Mila"* the Polish word for "pleasant" blended with the number eighteen, *"hai,"* symbolizing "life" in Hebrew, ironically designated this now empty Warsaw lot as a place of "pleasant life." A statue of the tall, muscular Anielevitz, the twenty-three year old leader of the Warsaw Ghetto uprising, stands where he fought his last battle for forty days until he was shot and fell, wrapped in what would become the Israeli flag, from the fourth floor window of Pleasant Life Street. One of the resistance movement's names he had chosen for himself was "Aniol," which means "angel" in Polish. The elderly passenger next to the window excused himself, in his heavily Slavic accented Hebrew, as he was getting off at the Mevatzeret Zion absorption center. Anielevitz ascended a burning pyre, only to descend, with the founding survivors of the

Warsaw Ghetto, a few miles from these palm-swept hills in the kibbutz commemorating his name, Yad Mordechai.

The wind carried the words of the Haifa graveside rite to my ears. *However he refused to be consumed by the Holocaust. His message was one of optimism. Although a major part of his life had ended in the crematoria, he believed that Jewish history did not. He would not concede to Hitler this victory. For him the state of Israel meant redemption. Have we learned from him? But more important, have we, his friends, taught that to our children? Will they, as the future generation of leaders, be able to follow through on the message of his life?*

WE WERE INVITED—THE WHOLE CITY
OF JERUSALEM WAS INVITED

WE WERE INVITED—THE WHOLE CITY OF JERUSALEM WAS INVITED

The sky was clear. The air was pure. The stars were bright. The night was still. The worshippers were in the synagogues completing the Shabbat prayers. The Wisnitz Hassidim assembled in the crumbling plaster shtibl (one room sanctuary) in the middle of the field on Hezikiyahu Hamelech. The young Dati (modern orthodox) parents and their children of B'nei Akiba affiliation, identified by men and boys, wearing small knitted kipahs, congregated in the Horeb Yeshiva High School off Tel Hai Street in a large classroom with long benches brought in for the holy day. And around the corner from the orphanage for girls, the Olim Hadashim (recent immigrants to Israel) blended with the well established Jerusalemites in the Hovivei-Zion Street synagogue, set amid picturesque villa houses, majestic trees, and carefully kept flower gardens illuminated by city street lamps.

Babar, Grimm, Anderson, Noddy, Hassidic tales and Bible storybooks were removed from the shelves. A mother Batya, a father Michael, an uncle Yacov, an older brother Zev, and a sister Miriam were reading with a certain impatience so that they could get out on time. Everyone wanted to extend his weekend a little longer except for a grandfather Shimshon, a grandmother Tenya, a great grandmother Leah, a great grandfather Yacov Yehoshua. They wanted to stretch the time allotted to them by the parents to be with their grandchildren and great-grandchildren, as did sister Haya who did not have a date. Nearby, the patients at the Hospital for Chronic Diseases were receiving their evening medication. Retired Jerusalemites, in knitted shawls or jackets, had not yet taken their evening summer strolls. Many were listening to their radios, waiting for the first newscast since late Friday afternoon after which they would turn off their radios and tune back into the tranquility of the Shabbat.

The stillness in the air was a prelude to the hustle and bustle of buses and heavy traffic, which would stream to the center of Jerusalem: Zion Square off Jaffa Road, King George and Ben Yehuda Streets, and small Luntz and Ben Hillel Streets. European films and Hollywood productions, the concert in Binyanei Ha'ooma, the large entertainment hall across from the Egged Bus Terminal, and the recently arrived Shakespearean Stratford actors at the Jerusalem Theater on Marcus Street— all these would soon set the stage for Jerusalemites on their night out. Meanwhile the waiters at the Khan Cafe near the railroad station were preparing tables for the guests who would come to hear the folk, jazz, traditional and rock songs of Arik Einstein, Yoram Gaon, Naomi Shemer, Yehudith Ravitz, Hava Alberstein. A few old tunes by Yaffa Yarkoni from the 1948 days, a few Biblical lyrics set to ancient melodies by Nehama Davrath, a song or two of Jacques Brel or Charles Aznavour, or a poem by Leonard Cohen sung at the piano bar might be thrown in to vary the fare. At the same time the disco dance clubs were preparing their blaring sound systems. The falafel stands, ice cream parlours, pizza huts, hamburger stand-ins and take-outs, and cafe houses were a quiet flurry of cutlery, scooping, cooking, movements in anticipation of the hungry crowds.

B'nei Akiba boys and girls were looking forward to their social evenings of discussion, folklore dances and horas. The Hassidim, sad to see the Shabbat go and reluctant to release her, were, nevertheless, looking forward to the Malave Malka celebration (songs and dances bidding the Shabbat farewell until next week) and to the words of their Rebbe's *drash* which would enlighten and inspire them for yet another week.

We were rushing as usual, afraid to be late. The dark, handsome figure of my brother was beside me. We cast our shadows next to the tall palm, thin pine, clustered cypress, unkempt Eucalyptus and bowed willow tree, whose shadows we were overtaking. The stark-white, stone apartment houses clearly contrasted with the pervading darkness.

From Rachel Imenu, we had turned the corner at Tel Hai, marveling at the arched, well-kept, old houses and along Kaf Tet November. We glanced up at the well-lit, third-story window with its decorative children's pictures and balcony with rocking horses, accoutrements of a private nursery run by a widow who had lost her husband in an earlier war and still had to earn her family's keep. The parents who sent the children here all agreed that few toys but much love and security kept the children happy. Further we went past the high school yard, where at this hour not a sound was to be heard, then along broad Marcus Street past the Jerusalem Theater on the left, up the hill past Windgate Square, towards the Prime Minister's Balfour Street residence, a white rectangular house annexed to a circular structure, where a line of people were entering for the afternoon and Havdalah service—an Open House, to which we were invited. The whole city of Jerusalem was invited. Of course, not everyone would come, but the invitation, announced by word of mouth and reported in the Jerusalem Post, Yediot Ahronot, Haaretz, Maariv and on radio and television, stated that just as the new occupant to the office had received all who came to the service prior to his becoming the Prime Minister, at his small Tel Aviv apartment, so would he continue to do as long as possible henceforth. The Shabbat afternoon and Havdalah service is a particularly lovely ceremony, with blessings in which a candle is lit symbolizing warmth and light, a spice box is passed around to smell of its fragrance, and wine is sipped, all to bring sweetness into the week, and I looked forward to the occasion. We were ushered through the door and the entrance, with its non-existent hall, to the dining room at the left. There we found a long table covered by a lace table cloth and the Prime Minister already uttering the words of the Havdalah prayer. His heavy, black-rimmed glasses reflected the flickering candle, which was a cluster of strands of blue and white wax with several wicks. By design, the candle revealed that it had been crafted in the Kefar Ezion Kibbutz, where in 1948 the mothers and children were evacuated but the fathers were surrounded and murdered. The sons and daughters returned in 1967 to begin the rebuilding.

The sweet smelling cloves and the Carmel wine were offered to the thirty or so milling guests. The short, balding man with greying, black hair combed straight back showed fatigue in his eyes but his manner was refreshed, portraying a buoyant welcome.

While singing the Havdalah, I heard a voice which faded when I was eight, but from my childhood its echo has remained with me. The *niggun* (melody) belonged to a white-haired, bespectacled, thoughtful kindly face of a grandfather who loved his grandson. The *Eliyahu Ha Navi* (Elijah the prophet) melody, sung to me on the telephone after the Shabbat if my grandfather was not with me, also had its echo. It is the song traditionally sung at the end of the Havdalah service. The song heralds the time when Elijah the Prophet will return to announce the arrival of the Messiah and the era which will bring about the end to war, suffering, misery, pain and tribulation, the beginning of everlasting peace, well being, joy, inspiration, fulfillment and understanding.

We thanked the Prime Minister, wished him a good week, bade him *l'hitraot* (until next time) and *shalom*. We walked out.

The sky was clear. The air was pure. The stars were bright. The night was alive. The Saturday evening activities had begun.

WHAT IS REALITY?
WHAT IS LUCIDITY?

WHAT IS REALITY? WHAT IS LUCIDITY?
(dedicated to Zev)

I saw him in the mirror. He sat there, at his desk, thinking of Jerusalem, praying for its safety and agonizing over a recent discussion we had had. I simply let him speak.

The Israeli raid on the nuclear facility in Iraq brought forward clearly what for a long time was not articulated. Somehow events, circumstances and situations which were related had not tied themselves together as closely as they might have. Coming as briefly as it did before the reunion of survivors of the Holocaust in Jerusalem, the raid underlined what the radiant faces, seen in person, on television or in the newspapers, of survivors, children of survivors (and in actuality we are all children of survivors), transmitted. More than a message of meaningful remembrance, they broadcast a determination, that we, their children, must never, ever forget; and thus a commandment to live and to ensure the life of future generations of our people until the end of time.

In what seemed a casual discussion with a friend of mine, in hushed tones over lunch in a quiet restaurant, a very crucial dialogue developed. "Are the present-day leaders of Israel, the generation of Holocaust survivors, realistic? Are they lucid? Are they not overreacting? Should it be they who make the decisions for Israel? Are they capable of clear-headed, rational decision-making?" my friend asked rhetorically. No. These men had been scarred, so deeply, it would be best for them not to lead the nation.

My argument was just the opposite. Because they had suffered so much, had gone to hell and come back to tell the tale, they had witnessed a higher sense of reality, or perhaps a lower or baser one of inhuman proportions. Just as some have experienced the highest peak of humanity, which approaches sainthood, others have witnessed humanity merged with Satan. Would we exclude someone from decision-making for having been the object of a great kindness, a true grace? By the same token, how can we exclude someone who has encountered immeasurable evil from being a functioning member of society? Who is to decide, in our violent terrorized world, what normalcy is? According to my friend's view, we would be obliged to create havens of peace, health and tranquility for future generations of leaders, where suffering would not be allowed, in order for clear, rational decision-making to take place. Could this be done? And would it be desirable?

I am reminded of the famous legend told of Gautama (Buddha, who founded Buddhism), whose aristocratic family was able to keep him isolated, secluded in its palace in India. Gautama's parents even ordered the servants never to speak of anguish, anxiety, physical suffering, ill health or death in front of their son. They were forbidden to cry or express any form of sadness before the young prince. Gautama grew up, and, until his late teens, had never observed the trials and tribulations of life. One day he decided to run away from the palace and see the world outside its sheltered walls. Thereafter, he vowed never to return to the false tranquility in which he had been brought up, for he knew that he could never again feel serene after having witnessed the tragedy and suffering of others.

Can tragedy be weighed? Can suffering be measured? At what point does trauma cause obsession? And is it obsessive, having seen one's world on the verge of destruction, to wish to prevent the experience from happening again? It is here that the survivors see risks, realizing inherent dangers which perhaps others who have not been in the abyss find it easy to deny.

My daughter, who is five, asked me, "Papa, why is there always war on the news? I hate the news." But she lately had said, "I want to watch it, I want to know. Explain it to me, Papa."

My son, who is two and a half, recently showed me a storybook entitled *Curious George.* It is about a loveable, cuddly monkey and his adventures. He asked that I sit down and he would tell me the story. He pointed to a picture of the monkey being carried into the air by an inflated balloon, which the monkey held in his paws. My child's creative imagination then went into action. In all earnestness he said, "The monkey will go up into the air, into a spaceship, fall down on the ground, there will be an accident, the monkey will hurt himself on the head, someone will run to him and kiss him on the boo boo and it will be all better." A story which could have had a sad ending had a reassuring one for my son who, thank God, feels cared for at this early age.

Some of us are not very far removed from the attitudes of children. Many of us, thank God, will remain as such when it comes to tragedy. But when it comes to calamity of the proportions of the Holocaust, yes, the minds of the survivors, their decision-making process, would have to have been affected. Had it not been so, there would not have been normalcy. The witness to the Holocaust would have had to have undergone voluntary or involuntary amnesia, an escape from his world rather than an involvement. Instead of functioning, choosing life after having been submerged in the depths of depression, sorrow, frustration and anger (any one of these or all of them), he would have kept his feelings buried deeply—without creative benefit to others and with destructive consequences to himself.

I recall something I witnessed a few years ago on a pilgrimage to Theresenstadt, the concentration camp in Czechoslovakia, where I went to pay homage to the fifteen thousand children who were brought there by the Germans to be killed. Only one hundred of the children escaped. The famous book, *I Never Saw Another Butterfly,* is a compilation of drawings and pictures by the children of this camp. During a guided tour of the children's barrack-quarters; the guide who pointed out the original drawings to us, stated, "As you can see these children were not normal. They were mentally ill after all they had seen, and their works show this."

I could not contain myself. I blurted out, "Dear lady, if you had lived through those times, and if you had remained normal then you would have been abnormal. These children show hope in spite of living in hell. They see a sunrise, a sunset, birds, butterflies and flowers. And beauty exists for these children, even though it has been exiled from the concentration camp. If they could see the marvels of nature and draw the pictures they did, in spite of having been so tormented, they were not only normal, they were in as perfect health as one can be, showing deep-rooted psychological strength in spite of their physical frailty."

Golda Meir, who had not witnessed the Holocaust personally, but who had experienced pogroms as a young child and the wars in Israel since the creation of the State, told an American journalist, "You say, I have the Holocaust complex and for that reason I am intransigent. I must be honest with you. I do not only have the Holocaust complex, I have the destruction of the First Temple complex; I have a Crusade complex, an Inquisition complex. I have a pogrom complex and yes, I have a Holocaust complex." After the journalist left, she requested that he return because she had forgotten to tell him "something of great importance," as she termed it. "I also have the hope of Yavneh, that in spite of calamity, all can be rebuilt." The children of Theresenstadt and Golda Meir met in their remembrance of Yavneh (a town in Palestine, where Jewish learning, and thus life, was able to continue after the destruction of Jerusalem by the Romans), a sign that although future dangers always lurked in their minds because of the experience of past dangers, serenity and hope could dwell there, too.

And this principle is not limited only to Jews. Are the Armenians who lived through Musa Dagh, the survivors of Bengladesh, the boat people of Viet Nam, the escapees from Idi Amin's Ugandan river cemeteries and the hunted of Cambodia, and, for that matter, the majority of the peoples of the globe who have lived through told and untold tragedies, to be barred from decision-making? If that is so, the world would have too few leaders. As a matter of fact, most states would have to be ruled by proxy by the handful of people who have experienced no trauma. And where would such people be found who are capable of ruling?

For those who have experienced hell and returned to tell the tale, who predict calamity and take grave steps to avert it because they see dire warnings while others see only a basis to discuss their preoccupation with the devastation which they experienced, all that can be said is: Can anyone truly say what is reality? what is lucidity?

THE SALON AND
"MY ROAD TO JERUSALEM"

THE SALON AND "MY ROAD TO JERUSALEM"

I woke up to the Piaf-like voice rising to my bedroom from the living room downstairs. Although it resounded more melodious and less full, the accent in English was a mixture of Paris and Jaslo, heavier on the Paris, yet charmingly soft. The piano vibrations held a resonance of treble, and I did not feel the deep lull of a bass. The lateness of the hour and the seemingly acute awareness which appears after tranquil sleep and tends, suddenly, to make of the child in us a philosopher combined with the richness of the melody to nudge an overflow of emotions into an all encompassing imagery. Suddenly all the pieces of the life of the person I had been thinking of came together, as if I had been intoxicated by an embracing intuitive comprehension. I sat at the top of the stairs and envisioned the scene.

My mother sat on a small, square, gold, four-legged, Louis XVI stool. The upholstered seat was flatly pillowed, sky blue, the same color as the rest of the living room, including the curtains, except for the gold rim on the moldings just below the ceilings. Being a child, it took me a while to realize that this living room was actually a salon and that all the other living rooms, I had seen in Montreal were not large dens without books. The furniture, paintings, sculpture, in the salon, like the inhabitants of the home, except for my one and only Canadian-born brother, had immigrated *in toto*, according to my mother's wishes, from our 7 rue Raynouyard, 16eme arrondissement, Paris apartment, across the street from the park from which the Trocadero and the

Champs de Mars appeared. The large ornate gold-framed, roco-co mirror, at the end of the wide, double-sized room, reflected the large chandelier and a white sculpture of the head of a smil-ing, little girl adorned in her braids. One of two Persian, blue-motif carpets which covered the floor was visible in the middle of the room, from its far side. A small yet tall, circular beige marble table, also gold legged with a golden ledge, was centered so as to allow room for a large Louis XVI chair, now noticeably empty, where my father often sat listening to my mother singing her songs, and frequently accompanying her by his harmonious whis-tling. In the mirror, a barely visible sofa stood in a corner-nook. All the material on the seats and on the backs of the chairs, as on the rest of the furniture, depicted colorful pastoral scenes inhab-ited by angels or young, regal, handsome men with their hair in buns and by dainty, pretty maidens. On the immediate, top left of the mirror hung a portrait of a fair lass embracing and being em-braced by two cherubic children. The top right corner of the mir-ror exhibited a painting of guests in a similar salon, although larger, which one would expect to find in a French palace; and a little further, the finest painting of all, from a museum, also in a guilded frame, like all the others, of a dark haired, voluptuous gypsy, wearing a red bonnet and a black dress adorned with crim-son, holding in her hands handiwork of flax. The profusion of red in the painting combined with the brown dancing eyes to give life, echoing a carefree, gypsy melody in the girl's expression.

The room streamed with light, which burst with dazzling radi-ance in the mirror, beaming from the wall lamps on either side of a large fireplace which was never used, but was preceded by a re-gal, break-front of material similar to the furniture, standing on four curved, gold legs. On the mantle of the fireplace stood an antique gold clock with a white face. The timepiece was centered between two, rather plump reclining angels; ever since I could re-member, I had heard its chime only a few times. To the right of the mantle, another large, Aubisson armchair, and in the corner-nook of the front portion of the double-roomed salon, a brown wood inlaid, finely polished vitrine with curved, bay windows displayed tiny porcelain, silver, gold and semi-precious stone wares on brown silk-lined shelves. On the left of the mirror, which could be seen upon entering the room, from either the regal, windowed double-doors of the front of the living room or the single wooden door at the end of the room where previously, there had hung a reproduction of the Mona Lisa, was a portrait of my gentle but strong, handsome, expressive, sad, blue-eyed father, who had passed away two years ago. Below the portrait, a rectangular, light grey marble table edged to the wall with a few mezzuzahs, some in a tiny white mother-of-pearl gold encased jewelry box with a Magen David and a few small prayer books with metal covers, of the type which are brought back as gifts from Israel. It was here that my mother would pray before she ate breakfast in the morning and before retiring at night. The mezzuzahs were lipstick-red-stained from being kissed. And thus each family member was blessed and prayed for, along with the world around a central prayer for peace in Israel. It was beside this table that my mother sat on the stool, playing the piano, immediately to the left of a round, blue cushioned hassock, where I often sat listening to her sing.

The small hands at the gold-painted piano were smooth, only slightly lined, with red fingernails cut short. A loose gold braid-stranded bracelet and an occasional ring were put aside on the music-sheet ledge to avoid clanking the keys. The short, but not tiny, figure of the brown haired, round faced woman with the small, finely sculpted nose, seemed to be one with the piano. Playing it was her way of relaxing, of entering another world, a world of yesterday, bringing it into her present and subconsciously, perhaps, trying to figure out the next step in the future of her two sons.

She was left with them on the passing of my father, her husband, when the present void in the house, suddenly set in on the night of the 29th of September, 1967, the 24th of Elul. Within a matter of hours, on the 30th of September, the 25th of Elul, my grandmother, my mother's kindly, also round faced, smiling, tiny mother passed away. It was my grandmother who brought from her large estate-home of twelve children, with governesses, Hebrew language tutors and piano specialists, from within a tiny village of the Poland before the Holocaust, classical music and the accompaniment of the piano to my grandfather's deep melodious voice. That autumn night had somehow linked itself tragically with the Second World War in Poland and, perhaps even more so, with the fact that during the war, my mother had been able to save her immediate family—father, mother and younger brother—and here, without a war, that had not been possible.

I remember the stillness of the house during the year of mourning when that piano was never touched. Yet my mother was determined to give us as pleasant and happy a life as possible, while providing all she could materially by frequently taking the arduous, business trips which my father had so often gone on. She was determined to maintain her healthy, positive outlook on life and to heed the order, given to her, by my eleven year old brother, who had been closest to my father, upon our return to our lower Westmount house from the hospital where my father had died: "I forbid you to look like a poor widow who needs pity."

I realize, only now, that from that moment on, resolve was in my mother, the same resolve which carried her and her family through the war. Looking back and now, I see the easy smile, the bursts of laughter, the more youthful attitude to life than mine, to which I have grown accustomed, the optimism, the innocence bordering on naivete, the fresh, spring-like creativity of character, and the selflessness. The calamity left much sadness but not a trace of bitterness. Her creative spontaneity has flowered in published books of poetry, over one hundred songs, music and lyrics in Polish, French and English, an M.A. in comparative education, a Ph.D. in philosophy, a meaningful philosophy of purpose which she teaches in a course entitled, "Ten Steps in the Land of Life" while being attached to an Ivy League University.

The radiant expression of awe, the illumination on her face, the sudden short silence which you know to be a prayer or a psalm of thankfulness to God for something, have remained. The youthful enthusiasm has not become the least bit tainted by her graduate education. She never dissects that without which there would be no poetry in life. A sunset has remained the same marvel for her that it was when her father, my grandfather, a writer, lawyer, poet of life, first pointed one out to her when she was a little girl traveling on a train to a vacation on the Baltic Sea. To this day, she points out sunsets, flowers, oceans and trees to us with, I am sure, the same child-like expression she showed her father on that train ride prior to the war, years ago. The child has remained in her; and it is this, that she brings out in us and others. Whatever is umblemished, fresh, spontaneous, disarming, continually surprising, touching the noble emotions, allowing the sentiments to be released, appealing to the finest of instincts her being evokes.

I recall a lecture which we both attended as fellow students in a Ph.D. program, given by Dr. Israel Efros, a philosopher-poet professor from Israel, a scholar well over eighty, a giant of a kind, gracious man. He spoke of Sadya Gaon's commentary on *Bereshit*, the creation. While everyone was taking notes, my mother had tears in her eyes, thanking God for being able to participate in such a lecture, appreciating the miracle of creation. Education kindles her poetic nature as it quenches that of others. In her travels to distant cities with my daughter, her grandchild, she steps into the historical, regal images of the furniture of the salon. She enters palaces, gardens, sprinkled with fountains, recounting tales of those who had once lived in these surroundings, sharing with my daughter the classical, background music of that era, and even occasionally springing up for a quick dance. She holds my daugher in those hands, which I, so often recall on the piano and particularly playing that song which accompanies me on my continuous journey to Jerusalem: "I walked, I walked, through life on my road to Jerusalem."

MY ROAD TO JERUSALEM

I walked, I walked through life
On my road to Jerusalem.
I walked, I walked through life
On my road to Jerusalem
through Paris, Moscow and Rome
through New York and thousands of towns
through the mountains, forests and streets
right and left, up and down.

From far away I came
Jerusalem, Jerusalem
I came here to pray
Jerusalem, Jerusalem.

They walked, they walked through life
on their road to Jerusalem.
They walked, they walked through life
on their road to Jerusalem,
through Auschwitz, Gross Rosen and camps
Warsaw ghettos, Treblinka and War
when they whispered, "Shema Israel"
on their road to Jerusalem.

They will never be forgotten
Those who whispered your name

who were dreaming about you
but who never came.
They live in the morning dew
in the clouds so grey or blue
and at dawn
they touch my hands with millions of hands.

From far away I came
Jerusalem, Jerusalem
I came here to pray
Jerusalem blessed be your name.

I prayed in Jerusalem at the wall
I prayed in Jerusalem at the wall
I prayed for the peace of the world
I prayed for the peace of the world
I repeated my old Hebrew prayer
which my mother taught me one day
and I wondered if the choir of angels
Prayed with me for every man on earth.

I prayed in Jerusalem at the wall
I prayed in Jerusalem at the wall
I prayed for the peace of the world
I prayed for the peace of the world
I was praying for Jews and for Moslems,
for all Christians, all Buddhists, all men
I was praying for those who were forbidden to pray
And my voice went up to Heaven
at the wall of Jerusalem
my old prayer so eternal for all my fellow men
at the sunset the sun was smiling
waving to me through the clouds
for a while I closed my eyes
waiting for the stars.

I was dreaming about people
joining hands across the seas
building bridges through the mountains
over hate and enemies.
And the flowers whispered softly
peace had come into the world
God was happy, God was singing
in Jerusalem at the wall.

I prayed in Jerusalem at the wall
I prayed in Jerusalem at the wall
I prayed for the peace in the world
I prayed for the peace in the world.
And one day when my dream will come true
men will never kill other men.
All the children will live without fear
and enjoy the daily bread of peace.
All the rivers in the West in the East
All the mountains in the South in the North
they will listen to God who will sing
In Jerusalem at the wall.

THE SUKKAH AND AVI AND AVITAL

THE SUKKAH AND AVI AND AVITAL

She was not yet two. It was Sukkot, the festival of the Tabernacles. We were sitting in the sukkah, my daughter and I. It was a sunny, pleasantly breezy, warm, early October day. This was the first Sukkot in Jerusalem in two thousand years when a portion of our family, as members of our people, would gather in Jerusalem during the pilgrimages of this, the Passover and the Shavuoth holidays. My wife had decorated our small, simple apartment-balcony makeshift tent with fruits, a few colorful portraits depicting the lives of the patriarchs and my daughters's drawings of the lulav and etrog.

We had finished a festive Yom Tov meal. While my wife was putting away the dishes and the remaining food in the kitchen, the finely proportioned, pretty little girl with blue-grey eyes and brown pig-tails just above the table as she looked at me, listened to a verse from the *Ethics of Our Fathers*, which I simplified. From the open siddur I picked a sentence, explaining to her that it meant she should be a good child because it was fun to be good. We would be so proud of her and that was enough; we did not have to give her something every time she had eaten everything and had behaved well at the table. For her concentration span, I thought I had finished my short lesson of thanksgiving after a sumptuous meal in satiated contentment. When she continued sitting and said, "Papa, tell me more," we went through a few more verses with examples, which I picked from the questions she asked. The sun streamed through the branches on the roof of the sukkah to glisten her hair.

A few years have passed. We are no longer in our sukkah in Jerusalem; it is now in us until we can build it again. It is bedtime. My daughter has asked that I tell her another story of Avi and Avital, a continuing story we have imagined between us. It is a bedtime tale of Alfredo, who is eight years old, and Alfredina who is five. The children of Giuseppe and Sophia, an Italian family, once resided in Rome for as many generations as they could remember. Giuseppe's father, a historian, killed by Fascists, always traced the family to the forced exile by the Romans in 70 A.D.

Giuseppe, a painter, dreamed, thought, conceived of Jerusalem on the many canvasses which adorned his tiny Roman studio until a wealthy American, connoisseur of art, discovered his work, brought him to Jeruslaem, and opened a flourishing studio for him in Yemin Moshe, next to the Montefiore Windmill. Alfredo, now proudly uses his Hebrew name, Avi, as does his sister, Avital, and Giuseppe and Sophia have become Joseph and Sarah. They live, work, worship and study in Jerusalem. Joseph has continued painting his scenes of Jerusalem in Jerusalem. The Jerusalem of his mind has, as he puts it, opened its gates to the strokes of his brush. Joseph's reputation was made after his first vernissage, a few months after his aliyah to Israel, when every painting was sold in one day. Critics consider his impressionist expression and technique most unique. As one writer has said, "He is able to combine the past and the present, Monet-like, as if the viewer suddenly sees a familiar scene for the first time, guided by that for which he is best known, his lighting effects' they, rather than the changing seasons, create the mood of each painting. His popularity is often attributed to the timeless quality in his paintings, in that they have a genre of their own, taking their cue from the Jerusalem landscape which melts into itself, wherein the architecture becomes inherent and part of the surroundings."

The adventure of Avi and Avital take them into Jerusalem streets, avenues, alleys, the Judean Hills and the hidden, inner courtyards which so few adults discover. When they are not in school or with their parents, Avi takes care of Avital. He became accustomed to responsibility as a young child in Rome, where his mother had to work. The paintings, which the children often saw in the Rome studio, enchanted the children; and for them Jerusalem then existed only in their father's paintings. Upon having first arrived in Jerusalem, they would rush home from their expeditions and excitedly exclaim, "Papa, it was just like the painting on the wall under the window, or it is that scene we saw next to the door." Although the studio in Jerusalem had similar paintings, for them that Roman grotto-gallery was their doorway to Jerusalem.

The months pass. Avi and Avital go to school, learn Hebrew, play with other children, visit. Their cirriculum, games, discussions and explorations become the chapters of the "head-stories" which my daughter requests before falling asleep to the lullabye, "Auf Den Pripitchike," after she recites the first line of the Shema and the Hebrew alphabet, "so that God can put all my prayers together in the best order possible and nothing is forgotten." But not before my wife, her mother, sings her "Numi, Numi." By this time, although she should be sleeping, she calls to me in the next room, then discusses another episode of her day which she has forgotten to recount. She gets up to show us a new dance she has learned, to the tune of "As Der Rebbe Danst, As Der Rebbe Laght" or the latest hora, which she has forgotten to teach me. To which my wife and I exclaim, "Please go to sleep; there will be time tomorrow."

THE FOG HAD NOT LIFTED

THE FOG HAD NOT LIFTED

The fog covered everything. An eerie spell had transfixed the moment. A perfect setting for the opening frames of an Ingmar Bergman film. The shapes were barely distinguishable, a few motionless forms of blended black, grey and brown. Upon approaching, I noticed four three-dimensional outlines under kafiyas. Featureless faces and non-descriptive hands floated in the thick atmosphere. A light drizzle made the stone-inlaid path from my apartment building slippery. I tried to brush away the sleep from my eyes but was unable to do so. The image, at first on my left before I passed it, and then on my right as I stared at it, appeared mirage-like. Yet it was real, but was it?

On my passing the caravan-stop, with the noticeably absent camel, the scene began to emerge but then to merge into the mist. The faces, for a few brief instants following my intrusion into their world, looked perfectly composed. I was bewildered. A small fire, which appeared continually to extinguish itself with drops of rain and the moist dense air, burnt on as if everything outside of the cross-legged figures around it did not exist. A small billow of charcoal smoke from a pipe distinguished itself from the light cloud which covered all of us, the rubble, the few blades of grass on what more often than not was parched earth.

I walked on, passed the chalk-white stone houses and apartment buildings of the Katamon quarter, which melted into obscurity. A clear memory came into focus. A soldier, he could not have been less than eighteen, although he looked as if he had put on his older brother's uniform, emerged from the Binyanei

Ha'ooma Concert Hall. With his Uzi at his side, he sat and listened to Rimsky Korsakov's Scheherazade being played by the Israel Symphony Orchestra. The myth and the reality became one. Scheherazade's tales, told during one thousand and one nights, were gathered through the emotions they evoked into an explosive symphony which either detonated with power and wrought havoc or were imbued with a sensuous, gentle quality bordering on ecstasy. The musical mist of enchantment encircled the spellbound audience in an aura which Scheherazade wove with her continuous tales so that her life would be spared. The stories had no beginning and no end. They just went on and on, with senseless killings, diabolical cruelty, with but brief respites of love and peaceful encounters. The force of magic and superstition reigned. Magicians, with hardware from the markerplace of life, cast spells and counter spells. Antidotes were found by bearers of hope and kindness, but not always; sometimes it was too late for the countless victims except for but one hero. The outcome was never known. Confusion was the norm. The characters were bewildered, lost in a mist.

I walked on. A distinct portrait of a cloudless blue sky and a Judean Hill panorama encircling a Jerusalem outskirt returned to me. Here stood a small, dark, black-haired boy with big brown bewildered eyes as I wiped away the remaining signs of a nosebleed with a fragrantly scented tissue from a tiny silver envelope with an El-Al seal, the souvenir of a long flight a world and a fog away. He had been punched and kicked after being teased by a stronger boy. He looked at me; I at him. He spoke no Hebrew, I no Arabic. He did not understand why I had stopped the fight to help him, but he knew that I had and it did not make sense. I extended my hand, he gave me his. We did not understand, why, but we felt it made sense.

I walked on; the fog had not lifted.

"I SEE THEM OVER AND OVER AGAIN"

"I SEE THEM OVER AND OVER AGAIN"

What is it about a Turkish bath that takes effect like a truth serum? Why do men suddenly expose their lives with such mellow ease and reveal their inner-most secrets? It is as if the warmth and comfort of the steam opens every pore, including every pore of the soul. The sublime profusion of mist sensually massages, slowly bathes and dreamily intoxicates all at once, releasing truths formerly imprisoned in silence; and words flow and flow, without beginning, without end.

He sat in a striped, multicolored robe which draped his long, thin frame, a Joseph recalling his dreams, realized and extinguished. He had brown hair, cut short, and brown burning eyes which bespoke a seriousness, sadness and comprehension far beyond his twenty-five years. Although youthful in his movements expended, he seemed to be missing some spark. An occasional hollow laugh emphasized certain pauses, but they punctuated his sentences like exclamation marks, rather than emerging as spontaneous expressions of joy. His eyes betryaed him even before his words did; the missing twinkle had not been exiled but had been clouded over, just as the hot vapour of the caldarium could not escape its windowless, mosaic encasement which we had just left.

Although several figures dotted the sleep-inducing plush, lounging canopies, lining the four walls of the large apoditorium, it was as if no one was there. Their voices were barely audible; only a mild scent of Turkish coffee and mint tea permeated our conversation.

"We grew up together, were married. She quietly beautiful, an open flower who gave me of her spring-like fragrance completely. Long, very long, onyx-black hair, dark, enchanting eyes, olive complexion, high cheek-bones, strong determined chin, delicate nose, graceful neck, perfectly shaped, inviting lips, small finely proportioned silken body. She had so many hopes, dreams. There would be peace, she said there had to be peace. We would be rich and famous. I would be a reknowned scientist, a Nobel laureate, invited by leading academies, kings and queens. We would dance in chandeliered, rococo ballrooms. The fact that I didn't know how to dance did not matter; I would learn! We would travel, visit castles in Spain, ski in the Alps, walk the streets of Paris, singing, sit in theaters in New York, hold hands, look at the works of Rembrandt in Holland, cruise the South Pacific . . . and if not, we could always dream, about such things and places, together. We would have a villa, surrounded by roses, built on a hill, on Marcus Street, just below the Jerusalem Theater. Our house would have a giant sky-light roof with sunshine streaming into each room by day and all the stars by night. Better still, one of my friends, Reuven, the creative architect, would design a home without walls; window panes would stretch everywhere from the ceiling to the floor. Thin curtains would dance to Jerusalem breezes. And, our children would pervade the colossal house with their laughter.

"She left me the images of those dreams in that aeroplane crash. I see them over and over again." He paused, shuddered, continued, "During the long months in the intensive-care unit of the hospital, I didn't know whether they kept me alive or killed me a little each day. I think both."

We walked out of the bath house into the explosion of sunlight in the Bukharian Quarter, accompanied by our silence and his again imprisoned dreams.

LETTER FROM A JONATHAN TO DAVID

LETTER FROM A JONATHAN TO DAVID

The 9th of Av 5741
August 9, 1981

Dear David,

I, or someone like me, once told you to return, that it was the right time, and you built the City of David, Jerusalem. I write to you now as your friend, one more Jonathan amongst the millions who have existed throughout history. I formulate my words as millions, I am sure, have in written and unwritten letters, asking you to return to herald a new era of everlasting understanding, wellbeing, contentment and peace. Do I know if this is the right time? I don't know. All I know is that . . .

All the breezes met. From the North, the South, the East and the West, from above and below, vertical and horizontal currents of air were swept into the Jerusalem landscape. With centripetal force, they were inhaled by the center of the world, true to the legend which ascribes to Jerusalem that distinction. And it is for that reason also that all passions are drawn to Jerusalem. The unbridled implosion of power is waiting, always waiting, to burst forth into a Messianic Era, a time beyond time when the City of Jerusalem will extend throughout Israel.

The whirlwind of characters in and drawn to Jerusalem, mine and those of others, some whose stories have been told, others imprisoned in silence, waiting to be heard and still others never to be told lest their secrets explode the universe are accompanied by millennia of melodies, shofar blasts, trumpet calls, battle cries, wails of morning, shouts of joy, whispers not audible, in the tumult, to the human ear, but felt, billions of words in hundreds of languages, accents and dialects, prayers, choir chants, psalms, dirges and a hymn of hope, all one. As if all that had to be said, was said, all at once, without pauses or chronology. What the mind could only comprehend by sequence, concentrating on one episode, and peripherally visualizing the background of perhaps other episodes, was taken in one torrent of wind. Just as it is said that the Ten Commandments were uttered all at once, so is all truth united, encompassed whole, where reason, passion, time, language all meet, transcending the limitations of each.

The prevailing Negev Desert sandstorms unfurled the Judean wilderness with grains which grew and blossomed into date, olive, fig, almond and pomegranate trees. Stowaway seeds carpeted the landscape with the color of white squills, buttercups, saffrons, crocuses, adonisies, cyclamens and narcissuses. Pine, cypress, eucalyptus and casurina trees endowed the landscape with their grace and dignity. The wind and rain chiseled deep ravines and canyons in the hills and rocks, occasionally contenting themselves with a gentle valley.

The Master Sculptor, Choreographer, Playwright, Painter, Musical Composer has reserved his right as Judge to intervention and final verdict, but has provided the possible materials, themes, music, lighting, sets, and scenarios for the choice which he has given his characters, most of whom have never walked the streets of Jerusalem, to either become protagonists or antagonists of·Jerusalem. The forces of good and evil, beauty and ugliness, sorrow and joy, comfort and pain, growth and destruction, birth and death, all meet, as does the fate of all nations. For it is here that the end will begin or the beginning will end as a prelude, or what may have become an interlude, to eternity.

I cannot speak for Him.

All that is left for me is to believe in Him and to . . .

"Walk about Zion, go round her, count her towers, mark well

her ramparts, go through her palaces, that you may tell a later generation that such is God, our God, forever and ever. He will guide us eternally.'' (psalm 48)

Do not tarry,

> We await you,
> one more,
> Jonathan